103Challenges

Manager-Led Wellness

FORWARD BY
Laura
Putnam

Judd Allen and Tad Mitchell

Thank you to the WellRight team who served as guinea pigs testing the challenges.Thank you to Renee and Tricia, our editors. Thank you to our reviewers. Thank you to Tamara who refined the artwork and did the layout. Thank you to all who provided feedback.

Judd and Tad

First Edition

Printed in U.S.A.

ISBN 978-0-9964417-7-3

More information about the book can be found at www.103Challenges.com.

Reviewers

Ralph Colao

John Harris

Jeff Klem

Christian Laplante

Brian Passon

Ryan Picarella

Laura Putnam

Mari Ryan

Foreword

Laura Putnam
Author of *Workplace Wellness that Works*

The evidence is clear: a healthier, happier workforce is good for people, good for the organization, and essential for building a winning team. It's no wonder that most organizations offer wellness programs. The problem is that, unlike the *Field of Dreams*, if you build it (as in, a workplace wellness program), they (as in, employees) will not necessarily come. In fact, as much as 80% of eligible employees simply opt out of workplace wellness, according to the largest study to date on the impact of workplace wellness. It's no wonder that we often hear: "Workplace wellness doesn't work."

I believe that workplace wellness *can* work, that we need to *make* it work, and that our best bet may lie in the promise of activating managers to become "multipliers of well-being." This is what my work has centered on for the past several years, and is the topic for my next book.

A growing body of research suggests that when managers become more engaged in their own well-being they create a positive multiplier effect for their teams.

Over the past several years, we have been activating managers across the country and around the world with a "leadership meets wellness" workshop. The workshop plants the seeds to start a manager-driven movement of well-being, but that's not enough. I am delighted that Tad Mitchell and Judd Allen have written a book that provides a much-needed follow-up to this workshop, along with other efforts to engage managers as multipliers of well-being.

103 Challenges can serve as a guide to even the busiest managers. More importantly, this book gives every manager the tools to not only stand up for wellness, but to become a better leader.

Prologue

This book offers 103 field-tested practices that foster a healthier, more cohesive, and more productive work environment. Unlike many proscriptive books on leadership, this is not a one-size-fits-all approach. Choose those practices that are best suited for your unique culture. Challenge yourself and your team to take a chance on something that stretches your current norms. It is likely you will find many of these practices habit worthy. Social capital and a good work atmosphere require your attention. In my experience, your efforts will be both fun and highly rewarding.

Judd Allen

Of the four wellness books I've written so far (*21 Habits*, *101 Challenges*, *102 Challenges*, and *103 Challenges*), this is by far the one that I'm the most excited about—because it's about helping managers become better managers which leads to better employees with no apparent effort on the employees' part. That's freaky powerful! Imagine wellness that really works without the normal hoopla associated with an employee wellness program. The magic is creating a healthy work environment where employees can't help but be well. You may be thinking, "That's not wellness." I beg to differ.

Tad Mitchell

Introduction

Whether you're a *manager* or a *wellness program manager*, this book can help you become better at what you do. It is different than most books. Instead of giving prolonged explanations, *103 Challenges* cuts to the chase and suggests specific habits to create better managers— which creates an environment that naturally fosters employee well-being.

How to Use This Book

Managers
Pick a challenge, try it, repeat. Over time you will become a much better manager, and you will find yourself surrounded with much happier, more productive team members.

Wellness Program Managers
Increase management engagement in your wellness program by including manager-specific challenges—fostering a strong and mutually supportive relationship between you and your management team.

How to Navigate This Book

The challenges are organized by primary category:

- **Purpose.** People thrive when they have a strong sense of purpose. Working toward an important goal can make them happier and motivate them to perform at higher levels.

- **Communication.** Everything goes more smoothly when people understand each other, and understanding begins with communication.

- **Mastery.** We all have the innate need to become better. The more this need is fulfilled at work, the happier employees will be.

- **Collaboration.** Not only can it be satisfying to work with others, it can create better results.

- **Environment.** The physical and procedural structure of our workplace sets the tone for how we conduct business.

- **Relationships.** Social interaction and companionship are extremely important for employees' health and emotional well-being.

Big**Picture**

Give some context

The Big Picture Challenge invites you to take the time to explain the context surrounding a work situation to your team. This situation could be a recent announcement, a reorganization, or even how your team contributes to your company's overall success. Everyone on your team will feel more connected and will better understand the importance of their role in the context of a larger purpose. A meeting format would be best for this type of communication—allowing you to instantly respond to questions or concerns—but if a meeting isn't possible, a conference call or email could work, too.

As a leader, you can see the big picture, but can easily forget that others in your organization may not. With only a limited perspective, others may feel their work is meaningless while the exact opposite is true! Note the story of the three bricklayers—when asked what they were doing, they had three different answers: (1) laying bricks, (2) putting up a wall, (3) building a cathedral. There is great power in understanding you are part of something bigger. Make sure your team harnesses this power.

Big Question

Create a driving question

The Big Question Challenge invites you to create a driving question for your team. This question is a lot like determining your team's mission statement, but it's much more tactical. For example, a hospitality company could ask, "What can I do right now to enhance the experience of a guest?" Similarly, a manufacturer could ask, "What can I do right now to improve the quality of our product?" Involve your team in the creation of the driving question so they all feel connected to it. Then print the question on signs to place around the office or use some other method to keep it in the forefront of their minds.

Your driving question will hopefully serve as a guidepost several times a day for everyone in your organization. Ask your staff to reference the driving question when making decisions and recognize them when they do. When someone suggests a potentially poor choice, others can bring up the driving question as a gentle way to keep them on track. The question will also start to define who you are as an organization and give purpose to what you do. So, choose your words wisely and get ready to see your big question applied to everything you do!

ChangeN**Tell**

Role model positive change

The Change N Tell Challenge invites you to pick something you'd like to change about yourself and share your goal with your team. Maybe you want to refrain from making negative statements or stop micromanaging your team. Once you've determined what you'd like to change, announce your goal to your team. Ask them to point out when you fall short—and maybe offer a small reward if they catch you! Don't stress about it if you're not perfect or even if you never fully achieve your goal. The point is to role model positive change so people recognize you are well aware you're not perfect but that you're trying to become better.

Change is hard. Perhaps the hardest part about it is recognizing that we're falling short in the first place. Acknowledging to your team that you're not perfect will be inspiring to them. It will reduce the employee—manager barrier by showing them that you are human, too. Like it or not, people tend to mimic their managers, so hopefully you'll end up with your entire team deciding to make positive changes in their lives, too. Wow! Think how rewarding that would be!

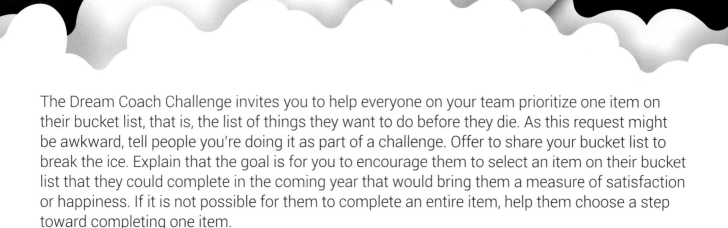

DreamCoach

Help people dream big

The Dream Coach Challenge invites you to help everyone on your team prioritize one item on their bucket list, that is, the list of things they want to do before they die. As this request might be awkward, tell people you're doing it as part of a challenge. Offer to share your bucket list to break the ice. Explain that the goal is for you to encourage them to select an item on their bucket list that they could complete in the coming year that would bring them a measure of satisfaction or happiness. If it is not possible for them to complete an entire item, help them choose a step toward completing one item.

Life moves fast. It's easy to get so focused on our immediate day-to-day activities that we let our dreams fade away. By helping people list their dreams and select one to pursue, you can literally breathe new energy into their life by giving them purpose. This exercise will also allow you to connect with people at a different level by understanding their passions. It's not part of the challenge, but it makes logical sense to follow up with the people you talked to and see how they progress throughout the year. Who knows where this experience will take you and your associates?

GoodIntentions

Understand others' purpose

The Good Intentions Challenge invites you to find out the personal mission of everyone who works for you. This may take a little work since most people don't know their personal mission statement. You may have to explain what it is, give them some examples, and give them some time to write it. When they are ready and you get together to talk about it, write their statement down to help you remember it. Ask probing questions about each person's purpose to help you better understand where they are coming from and why they chose that statement.

If you don't understand the why behind what someone does, you'll never understand anything they do. In fact, completing this challenge may be transformational for you as a leader. Things people did in the past that didn't make sense before will become clearer. Go forward, armed with each person's why, and you'll be much more effective matching people's missions with the company's mission, achieving success for both. Being a manager is sometimes like assembling a giant puzzle. Understanding everyone's purpose will help you see clearly to connect all the pieces in harmony.

GutCheck

Go with your gut 5 times

The Gut Check Challenge invites you to go with your gut feeling for five decisions that you need to make—big or small. Be careful, your gut feeling is *not* your first reaction. You need to think the decision through, do appropriate analysis, and consult others on their opinions, but in the end you should go with your gut. To get in touch with your gut instinct, you may need to find some quiet time—free from distractions—so you can clear your mind. Stop evaluating the options. Relax, clear your head, then listen to your heart. The answer will be there and you'll be at peace with it.

It's easy to get caught up with analyzing, seeking others' opinions, and running the options through our mind. However, this can lead to suboptimal solutions. Sure, we can blame the numbers or the expert's opinion if we're wrong, but that doesn't matter because we're still wrong and end up with an inferior result. As leaders, it's our job to make the big decisions. Successful leaders don't lean on others to do their job for them—they go with their gut. Say goodbye to indecisiveness and increase your "range" by taking the Gut Check Challenge!

Job**Hacker**

Help others job craft

Purpose

Communication

Mastery

Collaboration

The Job Hacker Challenge invites you to initiate conversations with those who work for you to help them job craft. Job crafting is molding a job in a way that makes it more interesting or furthers the person's career goals. It may be modifying a certain aspect of the job to make it more engaging or adding a completely new aspect. As a manager, you can be especially helpful in this process because you know what's acceptable and within the boundaries, and you know of possibilities your team member may not be aware of.

Imagine if everyone on your team was excited to come to work each day. That's the goal here. Think of job crafting as rearranging the furniture in a room or getting a new sofa—it's the same room, but it feels different, fresh, and new each time you walk in. You can help spark a higher level of job satisfaction, positivity, and even the quantity and quality of work in your organization by helping others make small tweaks or additions to their jobs. Granted, you most likely won't be able to help someone love what they do 100% of the time—this is work after all—but even if they can pursue their passions 10% of the time, it can have a huge impact. Think how wonderful it is to work at a job you love—and give that gift to others.

Look**Forward**

Help others create a 5-year plan

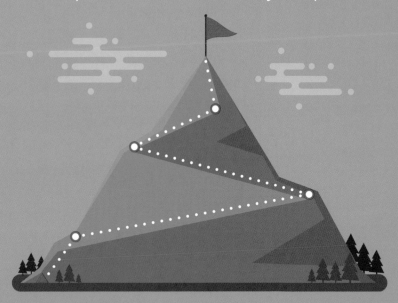

The Look Forward Challenge invites you to help everyone on your team create a five-year plan for themselves. Your role will be to give advice, encouragement, and moral support. (Consider doing #5 Good Intentions Challenge first—helping them create a personal mission statement, so they have an overarching purpose to start with.) Set up time to work with each of them and invite them to come prepared with a draft plan. Ask questions to help them validate their plan. If you have helpful ideas, then make suggestions, but be careful since the plan ultimately needs to be theirs. Your simple nudge to create this plan may be life changing for these people.

Most people don't take the initiative to plan where they'd like to be in five or more years. Your nudge may set in motion plans that will have a big impact on their future. From a managerial perspective, working together on a five-year plan may be the thing that turns an average performer into an all-star player. Or it may cause that person to realize they need to move on to something else to accomplish their goals. Perhaps even more importantly, giving your time to help plan their future shows you genuinely care about them, and that's a good thing!

MoonShot

Set a big, hairy, audacious goal

The Moon Shot Challenge invites you to set a huge, ambitious goal for your team. Maybe you already have a bold goal on your mind. If not, ponder the possibilities or hold a brainstorming session. Once you've gained the support of key stakeholders (or the whole team), put together a plan and announce the goal in grand style—you want to get everyone excited and on board! To complete the challenge you only need to announce the goal, but you'll want to follow up by posting the goal somewhere people can see it every day. You'll also want to track your progress toward the goal at periodic update meetings.

The moonshot decision was made on May 25, 1961 when President John F. Kennedy announced his goal to Congress to put a man on the moon by the end of the decade. Imagine the nation's delight when Apollo 11 landed on the moon eight years later on July 20, 1969—reaching this big, hairy, audacious goal. Just as President Kennedy's goal united a country in a time of turmoil, a visionary goal can unite your organization and inspire everyone to reach new heights. Start thinking of a monumental goal that you can accomplish together!

On**Target**
Set quarterly objectives

The On Target Challenge invites you to have the members of your team set between three and five quarterly performance objectives. Each objective should include one or more ways to measure whether the objective has actually been achieved. For some people, it will be hard to narrow their list down to so few items. This is part of the exercise. Consider reviewing each others' objectives as a team to improve the quality of the objectives and promote alignment. At the end of the quarter, score your objectives red, yellow, and green based on attainment of the defined results—then set your objectives for the next quarter!

Resist the temptation to tie the objectives directly to performance, so people can set stretch objectives without being punished for it (e.g., scoring an objective red does not equate to a bad performance review). You will be amazed at how much your team can accomplish when goal setting becomes part of your process. They'll be amazed too and grow to love the satisfaction that comes with accomplishment. Things may be a little rough during the first quarter as you get going. Trust the process, adjusting it as necessary to meet the needs of your team. Pretty soon your team will always be on target!

Peer**Support**

Set weekly goals together

Purpose

Communication

Mastery

The Peer Support Challenge invites you to set individual work goals in a team setting and report back. On a weekly basis—maybe in your staff meeting—take turns announcing one goal each for the week. On successive weeks, start by reporting on your goal for last week, then announcing a new goal. Consider having a scribe write everyone's goals down. It makes it easier to follow up. After a week or two, everyone will get into the groove and grow to love this productivity boost and the satisfaction that comes with achieving a goal together.

This challenge is not for every organization, but if it does work for yours, it can provide a lot of advantages. One is that your team will continually set specific goals, and they will be more motivated to achieve their goals because of the accountability and support they feel from stating them in front of their peers and boss. Your team will enjoy learning what everyone else is concerned about and better align their goals with each other. This can open up a dialog during the meeting or even afterward about ways they can help each other. Try it—you'll like it!

Purpose**Driven**

Create a group mission statement

The Purpose Driven Challenge invites you to create a team mission statement. If your organization already has a mission statement, that's great—build on it to create a more specific version for your team. If not, that's okay too—don't worry about creating a mission statement for the whole organization, just focus on your area. Gather your team together and ask why they do what they do and how it contributes to the company's overall success. With each successive answer, keep digging deeper into the whys until you find your group's mission. Knowing your collective purpose will help you reach greater heights. Make sure to post your mission statement on the wall physically or virtually if your group is widely distributed.

Purpose is where everything begins. Your company would not exist if there hadn't been a purpose to drive it from the very start. Don't settle with an uninspiring mission. A mission can have multiple good purposes including economic, service, and innovation. The purpose can develop and change over time. People have an innate desire to find meaning in their lives. If their job has a significant meaning or purpose, they will pour themselves more fully into their job, satisfying their deep internal needs and helping the company succeed.

Road**Map**

Create an annual plan together

The Road Map Challenge invites you to create an annual plan as a team. Get your team together and map out what you would like your next year to look like. What will you accomplish together? What tools and resources will you need? What other groups do you need to work with to be successful? What does your group need to do to make the company successful? You might be able to create your annual plan in a single meeting or you may need a series of meetings. Write up the plan listing tasks with due dates, or if you prefer pictures make it more of a project schedule Gantt chart.

Creating your annual plan together as a team is powerful. It helps strengthen the team and lets them know that you value their opinion. This challenge is a great first step. However, to make the plan real and effective, you will also need to review the plan regularly and measure your progress—if you don't, you will risk losing your team's trust instead of building it. As you complete the tasks in your annual plan, your team will feel a sense of accomplishment and anticipate the creation of the next plan. What will your next year look like?

Shared**Values**

Define what you stand for

The Shared Values Challenge invites you to create a set of shared values with your team. If your company already has a set of shared values, define some that are specific to your area. Your shared values will state the principles that define the culture of your organization (e.g., trust others, exceed expectations, have fun). You can use whatever process you want to define your values, but whatever you do, make sure to include everyone so they feel like a part of the end result. After you go to all that effort, make sure you post your shared values somewhere for everyone to see!

Having your values written and displayed for all to see sets the tone for your business. It helps create a social norm or culture. Whenever someone does not live up to the values, it makes it more acceptable and comfortable for their peers to remind them. It's amazing how such a small thing can have such a large impact immediately and an even larger impact over the long term. As people are naturally drawn to a cause, your shared values will make your business more like a cause and less like a transaction. What values does your business stand for?

TeamSpirit
Adopt a mascot

Purpose

Communication

Mastery

The Team Spirit Challenge invites you to adopt a team mascot that reflects the characteristics of your organization. Let your team help choose the mascot. Start by identifying the attributes you would like to exemplify as an organization. Once everyone is on board with what you'd like to project, propose mascots that represent this identity. Pick the one you like best or, if you're brave enough to honor the outcome, let the team decide. Once you've decided on your mascot, look for a figurine or stuffed animal to display in a prominent area in your office. Consider asking a graphic designer to create a logo using your mascot so your team can make in-house materials more fun.

It's one thing to merely say you want the company to be the fastest in your industry, whereas it's quite another to have a cheetah as a mascot. People can relate better to a mascot, because it brings life to the image you're trying to project and serves as a constant reminder of how you define success. A mascot also builds team spirit. Pretty soon you'll see your mascot popping up everywhere—building team spirit and reinforcing the key values of your organization. Which mascot will you choose?

3**Cheers**

Launch a peer-recognition program

The 3 Cheers Challenge invites you to create a platform for people to recognize each other. If your organization already has a peer-recognition program in place, publicize and promote it within your area. If not, devise a simple platform for your area. It can be as simple as having a wall where anyone can post a card recognizing another person. If you want to be more formal, create a form that people can fill out to nominate someone to be publicly recognized. Figure out what will work best for your group.

Recognizing people for their achievements is an important part of being a good manager, but it's difficult to do on your own because you can't observe everything that goes on. If you turn to your team to recognize their peers, you'll discover great things that are happening within your group. Each time your team ponders the good things that others have done and each time they receive recognition the entire team will benefit! Pondering the good in others is also very healthy. It builds a habit of looking for the positive (instead of the negative) in others. Imagine the power that a simple peer-to-peer recognition program could have for your team!

All**Stars**

Share what you like about each other

Communication

Environment

Relationships

The All Stars Challenge invites you to hold a session for your team where you all share what you like about each other. If there are more than 10 people on your team, consider breaking into smaller groups with separate sessions. Arrange everyone in a circle so they can see each other. Select a person to begin with and give everyone a chance to say something they like about that person. Encourage people to be specific, give examples, and try not to repeat what others have said. You can take turns going around the room or invite people to randomly speak up when they are ready to share something. There may be moments of awkwardness, but overall it will likely be an uplifting experience. Continue until everyone has been in the spotlight.

We often spend our time focusing on what we don't like about people instead of recognizing what we do like about them. This exercise will give your entire team a chance to practice sincerely looking for the positive, even in those with whom they don't necessarily enjoy working. It's also a humongous boost for each individual to receive compliments from everyone. It will propel them to continue working and living in that positive light. Start planning your All Stars session—it's sure to be a positive experience!

BraveHeart

Give constructive feedback

The Brave Heart Challenge invites you to give constructive feedback to three different people. You can give feedback on anything, big or small, but try to choose something meaningful that will help them excel in their career. Some things to remember when delivering feedback are: (1) be specific about the actions that are being addressed; (2) voice the feedback from the perspective of "my perceptions" rather than as a definitive fact; (3) refrain from using condemning language, such as calling someone lazy; and (4) feedback is best offered in private. Offering a pleasant smile is essential to any potentially sensitive conversation, as it shows you genuinely care about the person. If you're feeling especially brave, try giving some upward feedback!

These types of discussions with people can be unpleasant and disruptive, and make us avoid addressing problems. Yet, there are times when problems must be addressed and, as a manager, it's your job to do it. Be careful with the feedback power vested in you as a manager and find a way to be constructive and supportive.

Clear**Expectations**

Put someone on a performance plan

Communication

Mastery

Collaboration

The Clear Expectations Challenge invites you to put someone on a performance plan. This may sound like a drastic step to take with an employee just to meet a challenge. Still, there may be someone in your organization who should have been put on a performance plan a long time ago. Remember, a performance plan is *not* a step in the termination process—it's a tool to help people succeed. Once expectations are clearly communicated, most people rise to the challenge. This could be just what that someone needs.

It's important to involve the HR department when you are considering a performance plan. They are the experts and will guide you every step of the way—perhaps most importantly in deciding if a performance plan is the right tool in the first place. It's critical to be specific on how the employee is falling short and what exactly needs to be done to fix the problem. The HR department will help you prepare the plan, help you deliver the plan, suggest a follow-up schedule, and determine when it's time to close out the plan. Sound scary? This is a true challenge—but it's part of being an effective manager.

CreditDue

Give credit to 5 others

The Credit Due Challenge invites you to give five people or teams credit where credit is due in the next 30 days. First, think of five things that impressed you that you haven't acknowledged, appreciated, or given credit for. Think of recent successful initiatives and who was responsible. If you need more ideas, think of little things that add up to big things. You can also ask a confidant for help getting more ideas. When you do give credit, make sure to tell as broad of an audience as makes sense.

It's so easy to forget to acknowledge others' efforts especially when it's part of their normal job. Even worse, sometimes we inadvertently take credit for someone else's work by not pointing out their contribution when we receive praise for a team effort. Not receiving credit when credit is due is disheartening and can even lead to rebellion. Conversely, receiving credit for our work helps us own our work, which can take performance to new levels. Practice being aware of all the good that is happening around you and call it out for everyone to see!

CHALLENGE
21

DrillDown

Learn what 3 others do

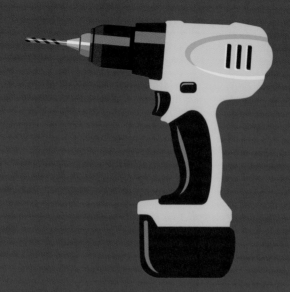

Communication

Mastery

Collaboration

Relationships

The Drill Down Challenge invites you to learn about what three people do in their jobs. Ideally these will be three people who work for you but they could be others too. Spend some time with each person figuring out which parts of their job would be important for you to understand. Then schedule times where you can shadow them as they perform these functions. It will likely take several meetings to understand their different functions and it may be awkward at times, but it will be worth it. Imagine if someone did the same for you.

It's common for employees to feel like their manager doesn't appreciate all that they do—often because their manager is not aware of all that they do. This is natural since the manager may not have ever done their employees' jobs before or it's been a long time since they did. Taking time to notice what your team does will not only help you better understand them—it will increase their respect for you. Also, with your broader perspective of upstream and downstream processes, you may find ways to make their jobs easier and more productive. It will be such an interesting process that you'll wonder why you haven't taken the time before!

Face Time

Opt for in-person

The Face Time Challenge invites you to choose an in-person conversation instead of an email or text for a total of 20 times in the next 30 days. Ideally the communication should be with someone in your organization, but if it's with someone outside your firm, that's fine. If possible, approach the person and talk face to face. If the person is not nearby, call or video-chat the person. Voicemails don't count. Try calling again if you don't reach them. If you're in a rush, keep to the point; it doesn't matter if the conversation takes 15 seconds or 15 minutes. The goal of this challenge is to take the time to enjoy the conversation and be fully present.

Email can be perfect for some communications—quick and efficient, but sometimes an in-person conversation is a much better choice. We sometimes shortchange ourselves when we choose email over face-to-face communication. It's healthy and helpful to interact directly with other people. We see their facial expressions, hear the intonations in their voice, and sense things we wouldn't through a text or email. Surprisingly, we tend to be kinder with our words and more understanding when we communicate in person—something we could all benefit from. Get ready to enjoy one of life's simple pleasures—a face-to-face chat!

Communication

Collaboration

Relationships

Fortune Teller

Help others see their potential

The Fortune Teller Challenge invites you to help each member of your team understand the potential you see in them. Take some time by yourself to ponder each team member and who you see them becoming. Focus on their strengths, not their weaknesses. Once you're ready, find a time to meet individually with each person to share your thoughts. Point out the person's strengths and explain where you see them going in in their career and/or in their life. If appropriate, you may even want to call out some of the person's weaknesses that they will need to conquer in order to rise to their potential.

Often it's hard for people to see the potential within themselves. They are so close to themselves that they can't see clearly, stumbling through life progressing slowly. However, if an outsider can help them truly understand their potential, weaknesses that were previously mountains become small speed bumps as they rise to their calling in life. No matter how badly we want to change someone else, we can't do it—they have to do it themselves. However, we can help others understand their potential—leading to a beautiful, self-induced transformation.

Get**Trendy**

Discuss industry trends

The Get Trendy Challenge invites you to spend time with your team discussing industry trends. It doesn't matter who leads the discussion or who talks the most—you may even want to invite a guest speaker. Get together with your team and talk about what's happening in your industry in general, what is going on with your competitors, and what your company is doing to address the industry trends. Finally, discuss what specifically your team is doing to address those trends.

Everyone on your team has a different insights. An open discussion can help you all better understand what's going on in the market. Having this context will help you all better weather the ups and downs of work and help you understand you're a part of something bigger—which can have a huge impact on your job satisfaction and ultimate personal happiness!

Listen Up

Ask for feedback

Communication

Mastery

Collaboration

The Listen Up Challenge invites you to ask for feedback from each person who reports to you. You can be formal and set up a meeting or just ask the person spontaneously. You can ask for unlimited general feedback or make it easier for you both by asking specifically for one thing you do well and one thing you could improve upon. When receiving feedback, resist the temptation to either downplay compliments or defend yourself—simply listen. Don't forget to say thank you and, if appropriate, commit to change right then!

Asking for feedback can be intimidating. What if people give you negative feedback? It's okay... you asked for it! Seriously, they're just trying to help you—like you are when you provide feedback to someone else. In fact, seeking feedback from others can make giving it feel more natural. It's good to know what you do well, so you can keep doing it. It's also good to know where you fall short or how others perceive you so you can improve yourself. It's impossible to figure this out for yourself; you need the feedback of others. Ask for help and accelerate your growth!

Major**Award**

Give an award

The Major Award Challenge invites you to give an award to an individual or team. Think of a person or team who has done something notable for the organization. If your organization already has an award program in place, use it. If your organization doesn't have an award program, create one! Order an official prize to give the winner, such as an engraved crystal award or a metal trophy cup. When you give the award, make it a big deal—present it in front of a large group of people and explain in depth why the award is deserved. You could even consider having a celebratory lunch or dinner.

Giving an award may not seem like a big deal for you, but it might be something the recipient(s) will cherish for years to come. Recognition has a great impact. People need to know that they matter and are appreciated. An award is like a compliment combined with a thank you—magnified 10 times! It demonstrates to the entire organization that you appreciate good work—and reminds them that if they put forth the effort then they could receive an award, too. Expressing appreciation through an award is beneficial to you as well. As you look for award-worthy achievements, you'll be training yourself to always look for the good in your team!

Marching**Orders**

Update your job descriptions

The Marching Orders Challenge invites you to create an up-to-date job description for each employee who reports to you. You can write the job descriptions and have your employees review them or do the opposite. Either way, it should be a collaborative effort, forming a type of contract between you and the employee—clearly delineating what the employee needs to do to be successful in their job. Don't forget to update your own job description and consider sharing it with your employees.

We usually only write job descriptions to fill an open position and then it is quickly forgotten. People want to be successful but it's not always clear what success in their jobs means. Most likely, a manager's definition of success is different than an employee's. This is natural since both have different perspectives. A detailed, up-to-date job description can help bring these two worlds together making everyone happier and more successful. Make it a practice to review and update your job descriptions at least once a year, perhaps as part of your employee review process!

On**Track**

Hold daily stand-up meetings

Communication

Mastery

Collaboration

The On Track Challenge invites you to hold a brief stand-up meeting each day with your group. The term "stand-up meeting" means that the meeting won't last any longer than you're comfortable standing (5–10 minutes) and ensures people are succinct and on-point when talking. Gather as a group (usually in the morning) and briefly review the progress from the previous day, the plans for the current day, and any foreseen problems. If your team is not all at the same location, you can hold a conference call instead. The meeting can be led by a single person or each participant can take a turn giving a brief status update.

Daily stand-up meetings bring the team together and make sure everyone is united and focused on the task at hand. Stand-up meetings can boost productivity tremendously—and boost morale as well! In today's world of flexible work schedules, it's a nice way to gently encourage punctuality and unity. Maybe daily meetings aren't practical for your group—that's fine, perhaps a meeting every other day could work? However, for many workplaces, daily stand-up meetings work well and are the norm. Could they be the new norm for your group?

PositiveBuzz

Give positive feedback

The Positive Buzz Challenge invites you to give positive, work-related feedback to at least one person in your group each day for the next 20 work days. If you miss a day, you can give positive feedback to two people the next day to catch up. The feedback should relate directly to their work, that is, not concern how they look, excel at a hobby, etc. You can be spontaneous with your feedback, but you may also need to be methodical so everyone gets at least one piece of positive feedback—yes, everyone—including that person who frustrates you! Go easy. If you overdo it, it will not seem sincere.

This challenge will help you create the habit of coming in each day and looking for the good that others are doing. Sadly, we often only comment when someone does something we don't like—which can be discouraging for the recipient—and it's not that great for you, either! Positive feedback does just the opposite—it lifts our spirits and boosts the person you praise. As you look for the good, the world amazingly becomes a better place even though nothing but your outlook has changed!

CheckIn

Proactively reach out

The Check In Challenge invites you to proactively reach out to someone each day for the next 30 days. Select a person who you don't normally talk to on a daily basis—maybe even your boss! Focus on work people during the week and family and friends on the weekend. Email them, call them, or find a place to chat. Try to think of some praise or some positive news you can share with them. Ask them if there is anything you can do to help them. Keep it brief. Make it an experience that they will want to have again soon.

Most often we only reach out to people when we need something or there is a problem. In relationships (especially boss–employee relationships), this makes people expect something bad every time you reach out to them, leading to an unhealthy relationship. The hope with this challenge is to change this expectation and outcome. Done regularly and properly, people won't expect extra work or bad news when they hear from you, reducing stress and strengthening your relationship. How great would that be if everyone looked forward to hearing from you?

ScoreBoard

Maintain a group dashboard

The Score Board Challenge invites you to track your organization's key metrics in a place where everyone can see them. The first trick is figuring out what your key metrics are. If you're not sure, pick some metrics to start with and revise them over time. Next, you need to choose a central place to post the metrics: a whiteboard or poster if you're all in the same location; an email or on-line message board if you're in different locations. Finally, you need to decide on a good frequency to track your metrics: daily, weekly, or monthly. To complete the challenge, post your metrics at least twice. Hopefully, you'll never stop!

"You can't manage what you don't measure," said Peter Drucker, known as the inventor of modern business management. You'll be amazed at what you accomplish—you really do get what you measure. Choose your metrics wisely, and the numbers will let everyone know what's important—uniting your team and giving them something to rally around and celebrate. Everyone will love to watch the scoreboard—especially if they're succeeding, so be sure to set realistic goals that allow them to succeed.

StatusCheck

Publish 4 status reports

The Status Check Challenge invites you to create and publish four status reports—perhaps one each week or whatever frequency you determine is best. Your status report can be as simple as an email update or it can be a formatted document that includes tables, numbers, and charts. Make sure your status report anticipates the needs of your audience, usually your boss or a customer you're servicing. You may even want to ask them what they find most useful in the report. Consider copying your team when you send your status report so they can see what is being measured and the progress being made.

The practice of creating a status report is helpful on many levels: it keeps you focused on what is most important, it helps you see the progress you're making, it proactively keeps your boss/ customer updated, and it communicates current information to your team. Status reports are one of those things you may think you don't have time to do, when in actuality, you don't have time *not* to do them! Take the challenge—status reports are a powerful tool.

TownHall

Hold an all-hands meeting

The Town Hall Challenge invites you to hold an informational meeting for everyone in your group. The objective of the meeting is to update everyone on what's happening within your group and throughout the company as a whole. You can do all the talking or you can invite others to give updates on their part of the business. The meeting doesn't have to be long—15 to 30 minutes may be plenty. To complete the challenge, you only need to hold one meeting, but hopefully this will become part of your routine.

People are happier when they feel connected and share a greater purpose. Holding an all-hands meeting fosters these two elements by introducing new employees, recognizing current employees, and allowing people to share what they're working on. Explain the big picture of what the company is trying to accomplish. Review your goals and any progress being made. Shut down the rumor mill by quickly defusing sensitive topics as they arise. What might seem like a waste of time to you can make a huge difference for someone in your group. Feeling connected as a team and sharing a greater purpose will decrease turnover and increase productivity.

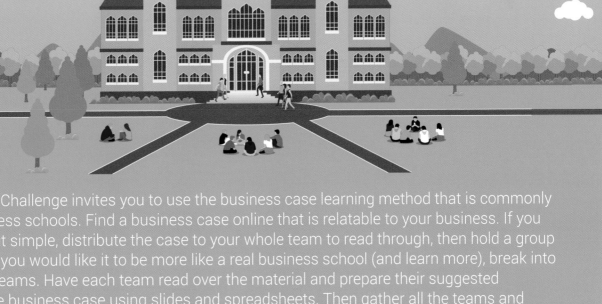

B**School**

Review a case study

The B School Challenge invites you to use the business case learning method that is commonly used in business schools. Find a business case online that is relatable to your business. If you want to keep it simple, distribute the case to your whole team to read through, then hold a group discussion. If you would like it to be more like a real business school (and learn more), break into two or more teams. Have each team read over the material and prepare their suggested solution to the business case using slides and spreadsheets. Then gather all the teams and have each group present their solution. End with a group discussion—comparing and contrasting the various solutions.

The business case learning method puts participants in the driver's seat as if it were their own business, helping them think and make decisions like business leaders. This can shift the perspective in a way that will truly benefit your team. Another plus for this method is that it requires collaboration—potentially among people who don't normally work together, allowing them to form new relationships. Each group must devise a solution and help in the creation of the materials for the presentation. Presenting the case solution will give each person a great opportunity to practice being up in front of others. Finally, as you discuss the case together at the end, you can apply what you've learned to improve your business.

BookClub

Read a book together

The Book Club Challenge invites you to form a book club within your group and read together. Pick a book that supports a current initiative or one that is outside your area of expertise to help gain new insights. Invite everyone to read the book, breaking it down into bite-sized pieces (chapters or sections) that you can discuss on specific dates (weekly or monthly). At your book club meetings, you can let everyone discuss the book freely or let people take turns leading the discussion. To complete the challenge, read and discuss the entire book together.

Learning is satisfying in and of itself, but when you do it with others, the fulfillment becomes more fun and multifaceted! Your insights are deeper. Your respect for others grows. You'll find yourself looking forward to your discussions. Learning from each other is also much more effective than just listening to a one-person lecture. Everyone can learn on their own terms at their own pace, internalizing and experimenting with the messages as they go. Hopefully everyone will enjoy this challenge so much that they'll want to continue on with another book!

Book**Learning**

Read a leadership book

The Book Learning Challenge invites you to read a book on leadership, management, or some other topic pertinent to your position. Search for best sellers, ask friends what their favorite management books are, or re-read a favorite that you've already read. If reading is not your thing, get the audiobook version and listen at the gym, at night, or during your commute each day. Take it slowly and enjoy the journey. One benefit from reading a book gradually is that you get a chance to ponder and practice what you are learning as you go.

Taking time to learn will help you solidify concepts you already know through experience. Seeing the concepts spelled out or having them delivered in a different way will give you the confidence to leverage them more often. It will also prompt you to share what you are reading with others so they can grow as well. There's always a chance that you may actually learn something new! The mere fact that you are reading a book about leadership will put you in a growth mindset, which is key for success in most areas of life. What do you want to learn about?

CheckList

Create a checklist

Mastery

The Check List Challenge invites you to create a checklist for a process in your area. Pick a process that's straightforward and simple, but also has steps that could possibly be missed— like a new employee training checklist. Don't overthink it. Brainstorm with others, if that helps. Write down any steps for the process that you can think of and add more over time if it makes sense. If there is a particular step that doesn't need to be done every time, include it on the checklist with a description of when this step is needed.

We do many things on a daily basis that are simple and routine; yet we never think to take the time to document the process. What if someone's out of the office and their back-up person misses part of the process? What if a big problem occurs and we never document the steps we took to solve it—and then we relive the exact same problem a year later? It doesn't have to be this way. Make your area more predictable and efficient by creating a checklist today!

Class**Mates**

Take a class together

The Class Mates Challenge invites you to attend a class together as a team. Pick a topic that you would all enjoy and from which you will benefit (mandatory training doesn't count). Opt for in-person training, if possible. Ask the instructor to conduct the training in your facility to make it more accessible to your team (plus it's often less expensive that way). A live video conference is another option. You could also ask someone in your organization to lead the training. If you can't all attend training at the same time, hold classes at different times or select an online course. The duration of the course is up to you.

Training is a wonderful thing. It pulls us out of our everyday routine and gives us a chance to stop and think. Even if we are familiar with the topic discussed, training solidifies the concepts and gives us more confidence as we apply them in our lives. Doing the training together not only builds team spirit, but also creates a natural support group for implementing the principles learned. Training makes people feel important and valued—and makes them more valuable to the company. What type of training would propel your organization forward?

Corporate**Assets**

Write down your team's strengths

The Corporate Assets Challenge invites you to list the strengths of every member on your team. You can do the activity by yourself, or turn it into a team exercise and take turns listing the strengths of each team member. Don't stop with work-related strengths—list other strong points and even character traits! You may even consider asking the person you are describing to chime in. Understanding how people see themselves can provide invaluable insight. Once you have the list, review it periodically to keep everyone's strengths fresh in your mind.

When we think of others, we often define them by their weaknesses instead of their strengths. We need all types of people with all types of strengths to build a powerful team. A team of people who all have the same skills and capabilities isn't that powerful at all. Identify your team's assets, put them to work, and imagine what you can accomplish together!

Cross**Pollinate**

Hold a knowledge exchange

The Cross Pollinate Challenge invites you to teach another group what your team does and in turn, learn from that group about what they do. The other group may be in your organization or from an outside organization. Hold a single meeting where each group presents for half of the meeting or hold two separate meetings. Bring in lunch or snacks since food always makes things more fun! The leader of each group can present solo or invite others to help out.

Taking the time to learn about what your colleagues do helps us become more understanding —reducing friction in the workplace. Also, learning about both the upstream and downstream processes can lead to better integration and increased efficiency. Sharing what your group does will create a sense of pride, satisfaction, and ownership. Learning more about what goes on in an organization is better for everyone!

Communication

Mastery

Collaboration

Relationships

EducationPlan

Help people create an education plan

Mastery

Collaboration

Relationships

The Education Plan Challenge invites you to help everyone on your team create an education plan to increase their general knowledge. The education plan can be super simple, such as taking a course, attending a conference, or reading a book. You can also develop a plan that could take multiple years to accomplish, but stay focused on the current year, identifying timeframes for each part on the plan.

We know learning is important, but work can get hectic and fill all of our time. Pretty soon two, three, or four years could pass without anyone in the office doing anything to improve their knowledge or skills. Also, individuals may not be comfortable requesting funds and time for education. Having a manager's guidance and support can make all the difference in pursuing an education plan. This support may be what makes them want to stay with the organization long term—and helps them be a better asset to the organization!

Great**Expectations**

Give 10 people something to live up to

The Great Expectations Challenge invites you to give 10 people something to live up to. This may sound confusing, but it's actually quite easy. All you need to do is think of something someone does well and compliment them on it—and do that for 10 different people. You could tell an employee, "You always turn in your reports on time, and I appreciate that." In addition to giving praise, you have also set an expectation the person will now try to live up to. It's even more powerful when you give praise like this publicly.

The inspiration for this challenge comes from Dale Carnegie, who said, "Give the other person a fine reputation to live up to." Notice the use of the verb "give." You're actually giving someone a gift—a fine reputation, one of the nicest gifts you can give to anyone. Be liberal with your "gifting" and seize every opportunity to build someone's reputation. Who knows? You may change lives as the people you praise strive to live up to the reputation you have planted in their minds.

Communication

Mastery

Relationships

MeTime

Meet with yourself

The Me Time Challenge invites you to schedule a weekly meeting with yourself once a week for the next three weeks—hopefully building a habit you will want to continue. You'll most likely need between 30 and 60 minutes. Create an agenda for the week with things like your top-three priorities, what you did well last week, what you could have done better, what you can do to be more effective in the future, or things you can do to make specific people more successful. Don't just list the items in your mind. Write them down and speak them aloud to help your brain remember and act on them.

Most of us would go to great lengths to help someone else be successful—for example, taking the time to sit down together and review what they are doing well, where they could improve, and what they should focus on. Yet, we are not willing to take the time to do this for ourselves. As a manager, it's not just about you anymore. Your effectiveness impacts everyone around you. You need to schedule me time to do self-reflection and plan your next move. Others are counting on you to be your very best!

NoAuthority
Lead for a volunteer organization

The No Authority Challenge invites you to be a leader at a volunteer organization. While it can be any organization (including a volunteer organization within your company), the important thing is that the people you are leading must be volunteers. This presents an interesting dynamic for you as a leader since you will have no authoritative leverage. You can't give them a bad performance review, fire them, nor even dock their pay because there is no pay! You'll need to use true leadership skills. It may take some work to find the right organization and you may need to get your foot in the door as a helper, not a leader, but it will be worth it.

As a manager, you live in a false reality. No matter how much you ask people to tell you what they think, you're still their manager and they can't help but behave differently around you. Although this is still true to some degree for leaders of volunteers, it definitely occurs less. Volunteers can do or not do anything they want. You'll have to master your foundational leadership skills to have success without the crutch of authority to lean on. It will truly be a challenge, and you'll learn lessons that you will take with you into the office and for the rest of your life!

Peer2Peer

Meet with an industry peer

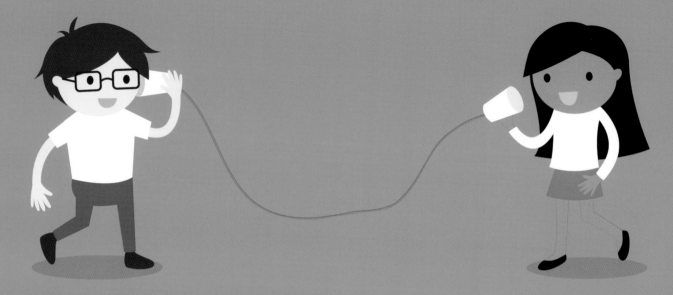

Mastery

Collaboration

The Peer 2 Peer Challenge invites you to find someone at another company who has a job similar to yours and meet with them. Hopefully, you will hit it off and decide to continue meeting, but for this challenge you only need to meet with them once. If you can't think of anyone, ask your friends and associates if they know someone, or try thinking of a company you respect and cold-call that peer. They'll likely be flattered and happy to meet with you. If you want to make the meeting even more productive, prepare a list of issues you are dealing with and invite your peer to do the same.

Like it or not, as a manager, you often find yourself on an island, left to figure things out by yourself. Most of the time you probably do a pretty good job going about it that way, but having an industry peer to talk to can give you support and the reassurance that you are on the right track. What's even better is that you can do the same for your peer. Talking through each other's issues will be hugely satisfying and educational. In fact, applying what you've learned may result in some of the most valuable improvements at work you've ever had!

PreMortem

Anticipate problems

The Pre Mortem Challenge invites you to hold a meeting with your team to anticipate problems before they happen. Select a product, service, process, or event and hold a brainstorming session to identify things that might go wrong with it in the future. Once you've got everyone's ideas listed, sort the potential problems by severity. For each potential problem, discuss actions that could be taken to prevent the problem. As a group, identify which preventive actions make sense to do and assign an owner to each of them.

Holding a post mortem to identify problems after the fact is a common practice. Why not identify problems before they happen and prevent them from ever happening? It's unlikely that you will anticipate all the problems you might encounter, but even if you prevent one the time and money saved can be dramatic; not to mention the stress caused for all involved. Make your team's world happier and calmer by anticipating problems before they even happen!

PostMortem

Figure out how to do better

The Post Mortem Challenge invites you to debrief after a major project. Consider inviting your internal or external customers, if appropriate. Before the meeting, distribute a questionnaire to get people thinking ahead of time. Include questions like, "What went well? What could have gone better? What should we do differently next time?" These same questions can serve as the meeting agenda. Appoint a scribe to document everything as you go. It's always good to start with a review of what went well. When you get to what didn't go well, avoid the blame game. Also, don't stop on the surface of the problem—dig deeper and deeper until you find the root cause.

Make sure you leave plenty of time at the end of your debriefing to talk about what you should do differently next time. Translate this list into a set of action items with specific owners so all your work gets put into practice later on, instead of being forgotten and the problems repeated during the next project. It might seem too labor intensive to do post-mortem reviews, but the reality is you don't have enough time *not* to do them. One positive finding can earn back the time spent on the post mortem many times over. Make sure you do them for every project!

Special**Guest**

Invite an expert to speak

The Special Guest Challenge invites you to bring in an expert to speak to your group. The expert can be from a different part of your organization or from outside the firm. An in-person address is optimal, but a web conference works, too. Find someone who can speak on a subject that is pertinent to your group. If the prospect of finding a good speaker seems daunting, ask others for ideas or suggestions. Once you have your expert scheduled, plan the presentation so there is time at the end for questions and answers. Remember: bring in food to make the event even more fun.

Taking time to schedule an expert to come speak shows your group that you care about investing in them and their professional growth. It will help them take a step back from their immediate work and think more broadly, possibly inspiring new ideas that will benefit your area. Sharing this time together will also create memories and a greater bond for your team. What will you learn about together?

Purpose

Mastery

Stop|It

Retire an unnecessary process

The Stop It Challenge invites you to find an unnecessary process or activity your group is doing and stop doing it. Things change. What was once a great idea may no longer be a great idea. Look for things you do that no longer add value or add little value to what your group does. Stop creating an onerous report, cancel a recurring meeting that is unproductive, cancel a subscription or service agreement, or empower your team by removing a burdensome approval process. If you can't think of anything, hold a brainstorming session with key people to identify opportunities. For this challenge, think eliminate, not improve.

There's nothing more frustrating than spending time and money on something that adds no value. By removing a non–value add process from your area, you will breathe the energy of hope into your organization. It will likely spur ideas on how to remove other inefficiencies. People will be happier and more productive. Perhaps more importantly, your team will grow to trust you more as a leader. What unnecessary process can you remove today?

StrengthFinder

Take a strength assessment

The Strength Finder Challenge invites you to have your team take a survey that identifies each individual's strengths and then discuss the results as a group. There are several strength surveys on the Internet—many are free of charge. These surveys only take 5–10 minutes; everyone could actually take the survey and discuss the results in the same meeting. Allow each person the chance to announce their survey results and share their feelings about the outcome. Afterward, take some time to discuss how understanding each other better can lead to a more productive workplace.

When people don't think and behave as we would like them to, we tend to get frustrated, but we truly need people with different approaches and strengths in life and at work. In fact, having people who are different on your team makes it stronger. This activity will give you a chance to recognize those differences and hopefully even learn to celebrate them. While this activity can be useful, make sure you don't fall into the trap of stereotyping each other. Just because people have certain tendencies doesn't mean they're that way all the time. Instead, use this activity as a way to learn to accept and appreciate everyone's differences.

CHALLENGE
51

SuggestionBox

Solicit improvement ideas

Communication

Mastery

Collaboration

Relationships

The Suggestion Box Challenge invites you to ask 10 employees for improvement ideas. Even if no one has any ideas, simply asking can have a big impact on job satisfaction because it gives people an opportunity to activate their brains and contribute to making your organization better. Make sure you set proper expectations by explaining all ideas cannot be implemented. Likely, some people will have to think about it for awhile and come back to you later with ideas. Receive all the input with eagerness and resist the temptation to shoot an idea down. Make sure to write the ideas down. When someone's idea is put into play, make sure to publicize it and give credit to the person who came up with it.

No environment is perfect. People will always be frustrated with something. What's important is that people feel like they have a say. If not, they eventually fall into a state of slumbering submission, perhaps making them easy to deal with but killing initiative and innovation—relegating your organization to mediocrity. Turn your people on—literally—and tap the power within them. Not only will your employees be more satisfied at work, your productivity will improve. What genius will you find within your organization?

SupportingPillar

Ask 5 people how you can better support them

The Supporting Pillar Challenge invites you to ask five people how you can better support them in the next 30 days. Simply ask each person what you can do to better support them. Some may be reluctant to give you an answer—ask again and assure them that you're willing and happy to help. If they still don't have any ideas, try a different angle like, "What can I do to help you do your job better?" or "What can I do to make your life a little easier?" You may need to give them some time to think and reconvene later. Write their responses down so you don't forget, preferably while you're still with the person.

Although it may seem like others around you are doing just fine, they often need your support but never ask for help. A seemingly small thing from you could make a tremendous difference for them. Even if they don't need your help at the moment, being asked will make them feel good and let them know that they are appreciated and valued. This will also provide the perfect opportunity to listen to their struggles and concerns—something that may be hard to surface in normal conversation. See what you can do to better support others and watch the positive effects ripple through your company!

TeamChallenge

Run a department challenge

Mastery

Environment

Relationships

The Team Challenge invites your group to do a challenge together. Pick an activity that will foster an attribute you are trying to build in your group. For example, challenge everyone to meet with a mentor, have an agenda for every meeting, or give positive feedback to someone in your group at least once a day. Whatever you do, make sure what they need to do is clear and achievable. Make it fun by having a reward for successful completion, like bringing in lunch.

Challenges are a fun way to get us out of our comfort zones to try new things we might not have otherwise tried—and maybe things we'll choose to continue doing in the long term. Challenges are much more fun when you do them as a group. The peer support can be just the nudge people need to join in and succeed. Doing something like this together also builds team spirit throughout the challenge and team lore over the long term. A leader like you can make this happen. What will you do for your team challenge?

WatchN**Learn**

Watch a video and discuss

The Watch N Learn Challenge invites you to watch a short, thought-provoking, or educational video and discuss it as a team. This activity could take as little as 15 minutes or could last more than an hour. Find a video on the Internet that addresses something pertinent to your workplace. Between YouTube and TED it will be easy to find something—and you'll get some bonus learning as you prescreen videos. Simply watch the video with your group and discuss it. You can prepare a short list of questions to spur the conversation. If it's quiet at first, just wait. People will start talking. Consider repeating the activity and taking turns choosing the video.

We all have an innate desire to learn, but we don't always have the time to take a class or read an entire book. This quick-hit education approach can fill this need and help foster a growth mindset in your team. It can also serve as a tool to remedy immediate problems in the workplace if you choose your video carefully. The activity will be a bright spot in a long workday, energizing your team to push forward. People will appreciate that you care enough to help build them as individuals. Hopefully you'll make this a regular activity. What will be the first topic that you explore?

Mastery

Collaboration

Environment

Relationships

1on1

Meet individually with your team

Communication

Mastery

Collaboration

Relationships

The 1 on 1 Challenge invites you to have a one-on-one meeting with each one of your team members. For some managers, this is already standard practice. For others, especially those who may have a large staff, this might sound like overkill. For the latter group, give one-on-ones a try. You only need to meet once with each person for this challenge, but you may want to set up recurring meetings for a while. The meeting can have as little or as much structure as you want and can be as long or short as you feel appropriate. Be sure to make it a two-way dialog, so you both leave with a clear understanding of what's going on in each other's minds. If you are in different locations, make sure to use a video call, not a phone call.

A regular one-on-one meeting automatically ensures that you are getting important facetime with your direct reports. Even if the format is *ad hoc*, it can be a very needed time to address any immediate issues and make sure your goals are in alignment. If you're already doing one-on-ones, try taking them to the next level by introducing a structured format that you follow each time—and watch the effectiveness of your meetings soar!

30/**60**/90

Launch a new hire

The 30/60/90 Challenge invites you to get a new employee off to a good start. Here's how it works: Meet with the employee on day 1 and define what success will look like at day 30. On day 30, you meet again to review their progress and define what success will look like at day 60. Repeat this process on day 60. You should certainly meet more often, but these monthly meetings serve as checkpoints to make sure the new employee is on track and receiving the necessary support needed for success.

People want to succeed, but don't usually have a clear vision of what success is—especially when they're just starting a new job. In fact, managers may not even know what success looks like for their new hires unless they write down reasonable expectations with specific timeframes. By taking the time to set clear expectations, you'll either accelerate the amount of time it takes to onboard your new employee or you'll quickly find out that your new employee doesn't have what it takes to be successful in your environment. Either way is a step in the right direction!

AdvisoryBoard

Seek advice from 5 people

Mastery

Collaboration

The Advisory Board Challenge invites you to seek advice from five people. Think of something that has been troubling you or a decision you can't seem to make. Now think of people you trust or who have unique insight or knowledge that could be helpful to you. Either set up individual meetings to talk about your issue or convene a single meeting with all five people at the same time. Remember, you don't have to take the advice; however, receiving guidance can help you weigh things out in your mind to find the best solution.

How great would it be to have an advisory board at your fingertips whenever you needed help? You already do! You may just not be using it. You know plenty of smart, talented people who are more than willing to help you—you just need to ask. They'll feel honored and flattered that you've sought their opinion and you'll get free advice. It's a win–win for everyone. What are you waiting for? Activate your advisory board today!

Relationships

BrainStorm

Hold a brainstorming session

The Brain Storm Challenge invites you to hold a brainstorming session. Identify a problem you could use some help with or a matter that's important to your group. Schedule a brainstorming session, allowing enough time so you won't feel rushed. Invite those who are either directly impacted by the problem or have some expertise or insight on the issue. Begin your meeting by exploring the problem thoroughly, then start brainstorming. Collect ideas. Write them on the board or on yellow sticky notes. Don't judge them—ponder them. Anything goes. A seemingly bad idea may lead to a great idea.

Once the group runs out of ideas, take the time to understand each one. Then narrow them down to the top three to five ideas. Vote, take turns moving the yellow stickies on the board, or whatever technique you like—just make sure everyone feels good about the result. Pause to understand each of the ideas on a deeper level and then try to narrow them down to just one or two solutions. Not only does brainstorming generate fresh ideas, it also helps build consensus in a group—something that's perhaps even more valuable than the ideas themselves. Who says work can't be fun?

Mastery

Collaboration

Relationships

BuddySystem

Set up a peer-mentoring system

The Buddy System Challenge invites you to create a peer-mentoring program within your group. This can take any form you like, but it's meant to be leadership directed. For example, you could pair each junior person with a more senior peer; or match people with someone who has a skill they need. They should meet regularly to talk about how things are going and help each other on an *ad hoc* basis. This not only frees up your time, but it also provides leadership opportunities for your senior staff and more nurturing help for your junior staff. However you decide to set up your buddy system, follow up to make sure it's working, adjusting pairs as necessary.

Mentoring has many forms. If you're uncomfortable calling this "mentoring" because you are the one who selected the pairs, perhaps you could call it partnering, coaching, or guiding. No matter what you call it, this system has the potential to benefit everyone involved, including you and your organization. The junior/senior pairs will help those involved feel important and provide a supportive environment. As reaching out to a boss can be intimidating, a senior mentor can provide a nurturing, positive relationship wherein a junior staffer can grow.

CustomerCall

Talk to a customer

The Customer Call Challenge invites you to arrange for one of your customers to come talk to your group. It would be ideal to meet with the customer in person, but a video chat or a conference call would also work. Ask the customer to explain why they use your product or service, how they use it, and how their experience with your product or organization could be better. The session doesn't have to be long, but make sure to leave some time for questions. You may even want to ask your team to prepare questions in advance. If talking with a customer isn't possible, find someone in your business who specializes in customer relationships instead.

In today's specialized world, many of us deliver products or services for customers we've never even met. Not only is it hard for us to build a customer-centric product having never met the customer, it's also demoralizing for us because we can't see how what we do fits into the world. Connecting your customers with your group will give a sense of meaning to everyone involved. Your customers will appreciate the attention, too!

Design**Review**

Review a deliverable

The Design Review Challenge invites you to review a document or other deliverable as a group. Model the way by choosing one of your deliverables. Set up a meeting to review the document with key players and others who could learn from the process. Distribute the document prior to the meeting with instructions for everyone to review it before you meet and highlight any areas of concern. Ask someone to moderate the meeting and another person to take notes (preferably not the author for either assignment). As each area of concern is discussed, determine as a group whether to classify it as a suggestion or an error that must be addressed by the author.

Two heads are better than one, and several are better than two. Design reviews are a great way to increase the quality of your deliverables, which in turn will increase the quality of downstream products. The review process can educate your team and provide an opportunity to gain consensus. As people take ownership in improving the organization's output, they will become more unified as a team. You only need to review one deliverable to complete this challenge, but hopefully you'll want to do it again and see what design reviews can do for your group!

FirstImpression

Solicit ideas from a new hire

The First Impression Challenge invites you to have a conversation with someone who is new to your organization. Schedule a formal meeting or grab lunch together—whatever suits your style. Use this as an opportunity to welcome the new person into the organization and get better acquainted. During your time together, ask some questions like: "What were your first impressions about the organization?" or "What can the organization do to better support you in your job?" Ask for specifics and come prepared to take notes; this will help you remember details later on and show the new hire that you value the input.

New people in a company have an extremely valuable perspective that only lasts a short time. They have been there long enough to understand how things work, but not long enough to become *accustomed* to how things work. This makes them ideal sources for how to improve things. Sure, not all of their ideas will make sense, but just a single idea may make a huge difference. Even if nothing comes of the meeting, you've at least met someone new and welcomed them into the organization!

Communication

Mastery

Collaboration

Relationships

Party Time

Form a fun committee

The Party Time Challenge invites you to organize a fun committee—a small group whose only aim is to plan fun events for the office. When you choose a chairperson, look for someone who will ensure these events are indeed F-U-N! The new chair can invite specific coworkers to be on the committee or can simply ask for volunteers. Let the chair know how often to host events, what kind of a budget is available, and if there are any particular events you wish to have (e.g., an event that includes friends and family). Then get out of the way and let them make it happen.

A fun committee is a great tool for initiating team-building activities. Giving others a chance to lead and plan events takes a burden off of you as well. Taking time to relax and socialize with your coworkers—while it might not seem like the best use of time—pays generous dividends, including decreasing stress and boosting morale. The more employees enjoy being together, the smoother things will go at work, especially when the going gets rough. Plus, it really can be a lot of fun!

SharedPower

Create a committee

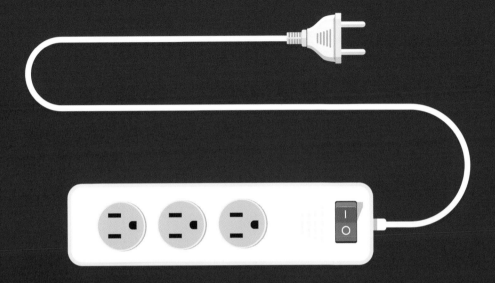

The Shared Power Challenge invites you to create a committee to handle an ongoing initiative or a one-time deliverable. Invite someone with high potential to chair the committee and then let that person recruit other committee members. Be clear whether you are asking for input or handing over decision-making authority. You may also want to identify what resources, if any, are likely to be available for the committee's work. You can count this challenge complete after the committee has its first meeting.

Committees are a great way to delegate work. They empower a whole group of people instead of an individual—and a group is much less likely to get off course than an individual. Generally, committee participation is voluntary, increasing buy-in. Once the committee figures out its approach, a ready-made team can execute the plan. One of the few things that can break the committee model is you, the sponsor. Make sure the boundaries are clear up front and then let the committee do its job. Nothing is more aggravating than having your ideas overridden by the sponsor. Trust the process and reap the benefits!

Collaboration

Relationships

StressTest

Ask how you stress people

The Stress Test Challenge invites you to ask the people who report to you how you stress them out. You may think that you don't, but think again. Does *your* boss stress you out? Probably. In fact, you stress your people out, too; the trick is getting them to open up and tell you how. You may need to ask several times in different ways or seed the discussion by bringing up things that others have mentioned. Once they start talking, don't get defensive. Listen and write their answers down; doing so will demonstrate your desire to understand how you affect them.

There's a natural tension between an employee and a boss. After all, your boss can fire you or even worse: make your life miserable. Think about the stress your boss causes you. Do you want to do the same to the people who work for you? Most bosses have no idea how they cause stress for their employees. Once you find out, create a list and read it periodically. After a couple of months, ask again. Even if the stress cannot be completely eliminated, your employees will feel better simply knowing that you care enough to ask.

Tongue Tied

Hold a meeting where you can't talk

The Tongue Tied Challenge invites you to hold a meeting to gather feedback. The unique aspect of this challenge is that you attend the meeting, but you cannot talk. You cannot say a single word. So make sure it's a topic where your feedback is not essential. Appoint someone beforehand to facilitate. Schedule the meeting with plenty of time as it may take awhile for the group to warm up. Explain why you are not talking, and then stop talking! Try not to express your opinions through your facial expressions as they speak—instead, keep a cheery disposition. Try to sit apart from the group or, for a little fun, wear a sign that indicates you will not be speaking.

As a manager, people sometimes put your words above others—if you can't talk, then it puts everyone on the same equal playing field. Your silence in this meeting will force the participants to generate their own thoughts and speak up—something they may not be used to. Your willingness to be silent will show the group you really do want to hear their opinions. It can be scary for you as a manager to relinquish control. It makes you vulnerable, but that's an attribute you need to better relate to others. Give this challenge a try and see what others have to say!

Top**Performer**

Coach your best employee

The Top Performer Challenge invites you to spend four hours with your best employee, coaching your top performer to become even better. It can be one four-hour meeting or several shorter meetings. Instead of being in the manager mindset, trying to correct deficiencies, get into the coaching mindset. Encourage them to continue doing more of what they're already doing well and to figure out ways to improve their weak areas. Don't try to change them; build confidence and pump them up like a coach would. Success begins in the mind! You may also take the opportunity to understand what you can do better to keep them engaged.

Managers often spend their time dealing with problem employees, leaving the top employees to fend for themselves. After all, the top employees already know what they are doing, right? Probably, but consider how much your area's output would improve if you invested four hours in your best employee instead of spending four hours with your lowest performer. This challenge will give you a chance to find out for yourself. Not only will you be pleased with your results, you'll also get to enjoy working more closely with your top talent. Hopefully, you'll want to continue coaching them even after this challenge is complete!

You're**It**

Delegate 10 tasks

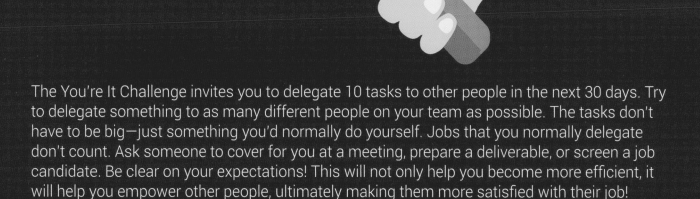

The You're It Challenge invites you to delegate 10 tasks to other people in the next 30 days. Try to delegate something to as many different people on your team as possible. The tasks don't have to be big—just something you'd normally do yourself. Jobs that you normally delegate don't count. Ask someone to cover for you at a meeting, prepare a deliverable, or screen a job candidate. Be clear on your expectations! This will not only help you become more efficient, it will help you empower other people, ultimately making them more satisfied with their job!

As leaders, we sometimes feel like we need to do everything ourselves. Sure, it's good to serve those you lead, but there needs to be some balance—you're a leader after all! Sharing work with others not only relieves you from a burden—it provides an opportunity for others to shine and shows them that you believe in them. Be careful though: It's not always easy to trust others—and trust is exactly what you'll need because employees might get turned off if you start meddling in a task you've assigned to them. Take a leap of faith and see how delegating can improve your life and the lives of others.

Collaboration

ArtGallery
Post family artwork

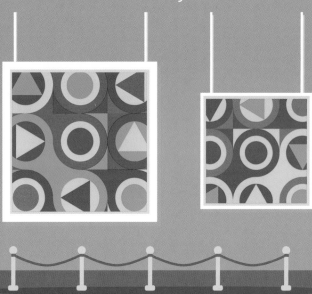

The Art Gallery Challenge invites you to set aside an area in your workplace to display the artwork of coworkers and their families. Children may end up being the biggest contributors, but you can certainly encourage team members and their mature family members to contribute too. Go all out and professionally frame the artwork to make it look exceptionally nice or get some low-cost frames and do it yourself. Consider including other types of art like poems and photo art. Mount a title on the wall so visitors understand what it is.

Art soothes the soul and stimulates the mind. In addition to beautifying your office, displaying family artwork will fulfill a deeper purpose. It will spur conversations and help employees get to know each other on a deeper level. The family art exhibit will create a sense of wholeness in the office, revealing that there's more to life than work; that the world is a beautiful place; that creating is human; and that employees are fathers, mothers, sons, and daughters who work to provide for their families. Bring this sense of humanity and unity to your office.

Environment

Relationships

Be**Real**

Do something silly

The Be Real Challenge invites you to do something silly or out of the ordinary. It doesn't have to be extreme, just something that most people wouldn't expect from you. Wear a funny hat or wig. Dress up in a costume for the day. Read a poem you've written to drive home a point. Stage a competition with someone else on the team. Whatever you do, try to choose something that will create memories and break down barriers with your team. If you can't think of a silly idea, ask a friend.

Like it or not, managers are in a different zone. Employees can't relate with them in the same way they do with others on their same level. It may seem impossible to change this, but it is possible to narrow the divide. By doing something silly, you're narrowing that gap and are demonstrating that you're a real person, too. You're also building memories—creating a sort of corporate lore that brings the team together. You only have to do one silly thing to complete this challenge, but make it memorable! Hopefully you'll continue to be silly every once in a while to better connect with your team.

Environment

Relationships

CelebrationTime

Celebrate an accomplishment

The Celebration Time Challenge invites you to celebrate a significant accomplishment of your team. Think of something really great your team has recently completed—one of your top accomplishments of the year. Then plan a fun way to celebrate! It could be as simple as bringing in pizza or going out for drinks, but it will be much more memorable and impactful if you do something more creative like hiring a masseuse to visit the office for a day, giving out movie tickets, or ordering custom t-shirts for everyone.

Too often we accomplish major feats but don't take the time to recognize and reward our team before we race off to our next task. Taking a moment to look back and realize that you're making progress is powerful. It can turn what seems like an endless march into a grand journey. Celebrating as a team also provides an opportunity to build relationships and create memories, which will spill over into making your organization even more efficient for the next accomplishment. Find a reason to celebrate and make it epic!

Environment

Relationships

CleanHouse

Hold an office clean-up day

The Clean House Challenge invites you to hold an office clean-up day. Designate a day for clean up and be sure everyone knows about it in advance so they can be in the office and not out for appointments. On the chosen day, set a specific time or let people choose a time that works best for them. Provide desk cleaner, paper towels, and extra trash bags. Go big and declutter while you're at it—remove excess or undesirable furniture, equipment, and whatever else clutters the office. Consider donating usable items to a local non-profit organization.

A clean workspace can help your team focus on their work and produce higher quality output. Having a clean area in which to work shows your team cares about their jobs and performance. Perhaps more importantly, this clean-up project will provide a chance for your team to do something together, build relationships, and build confidence that their combined efforts can accomplish great things! Clean feels good. Bring this positive feeling to your work environment.

Environment

Email Policy

Reduce email frustration

The Email Policy Challenge invites you to create an email policy. The policy should set the expectations around email etiquette, without creating too many rules. For instance, the policy may teach good email manners like don't reply to all when it is not necessary. In addition, the policy should allow each person the right to set their own personal boundaries. For example, if one person likes to send emails in the evening because it makes them sleep better, that is fine; but if another person does not like to read or respond to emails after work hours, supervisors are required to honor that.

Email is such a powerful tool, yet can be such a distraction at the same time—at work and at home. The goal of this challenge is to reduce the distraction factor, increasing efficiency and decreasing stress. With technology at our fingertips, one of the biggest frustrations about email for some is that they never get a chance to disconnect and recharge. Thus, allowing people to create their own email personal boundaries is a critical part of the email policy—and how this is accomplished will be different for each organization. Imagine how nice email would be if everyone played by a few simple rules!

Fresh**Perspective**

Take a break from the routine

The Fresh Perspective Challenge invites you to change things up and do something different in your team's daily routine. Hold a meeting outside. Play a game together. Go for a group walk. Play music in the office while you work. Get creative so it truly feels like a refreshing break from the normal day-to-day activities. The more creative the idea, the more memorable it will be for everyone. If creativity is not your strength, recruit others to drum up ideas and put them into play. If at all possible, get outside so fresh air is part of the experience!

Our brain loves patterns. It recognizes a pattern and creates an automatic response for it—sort of like a habit loop. If everything you experience is expected, then your brain stays on autopilot all day and doesn't need to work very hard. By switching things up, you can stimulate the brain—awakening it to a new level. This will not only make your workday more interesting, it will also make you and your team more effective. Breaking from the workday routine may be just the boost your team needs!

Environment

Relationships

Good**Practice**

Start a tradition

The Good Practice Challenge invites you to start a new tradition for your group. It can be a simple tradition, but make sure it's something that adds fun or brings unity to the team. Ring a bell when you close a deal. Go out for drinks every third "Thirstday." Decorate the desk of the office birthday girl (or guy). Choose the tradition yourself or ask your team for ideas. Hopefully the tradition will last and everyone will enjoy it, but if it does fizzle out, try to think of a new tradition that will continue on.

Traditions bring us together and give us something to anticipate and enjoy in a good way. Think of a holiday you look forward to each year. The anticipation makes life more fun and the special things you do around the holidays become a part of you. Traditions are simple, yet so powerful at the same time. Imagine creating a workplace that is productive, fun, and full of people who enjoy coming to work each day. That's the goal here—creating a better workplace sparked by a unifying tradition.

Environment

Relationships

GoodbyeFriday

Wish everyone a nice weekend

WEEKEND

..LOADING..

The Goodbye Friday Challenge invites you to go around the office on Friday afternoon and tell everyone to have a nice weekend—three Fridays in a row. Ideally you'll do this right before you leave (signaling that it's okay for them to leave also), but if you are staying late you'll need to make the rounds earlier so you can see everyone before they leave. If you have time, ask what their weekend plans are. Compliment them on their work for the week. Remember to smile so you send everyone off to their weekend with a burst of positive energy. To complete the challenge, do this three Fridays in a row—hopefully building a habit in the process. Create a recurring meeting on your calendar if you need a reminder.

Taking time to say goodbye and wish everyone a good weekend shows your employees you respect them, you enjoy working with them, and you understand that it's important for them to take a break and relax on the weekend. It's a net-positive interaction that will balance out the more stressful work-related interactions you have with people. Depending on how large your group is, this may be the only time during the week that you interact with some people. So take this simple opportunity to brighten your day and the Friday of those around you.

Environment

Relationships

GreenOffice

Help the environment

The Green Office Challenge invites you to help your office become more environmentally friendly. Go back to drip-brew coffee. Use real coffee mugs. Cut back on printing. Print on both sides of the paper. Add recycle bins. Drink water from reusable bottles. Perhaps there has already been a suggestion for change—all you need to do is implement it. It just takes a leader, and you are that leader. Make the change and, even if there are a few grumbles along the way, it will soon become the new normal. You only need to make one change to complete the challenge.

People love to feel like they are doing something good in the world and helping the environment is a simple way to collectively make an impact. Take advantage of the willing hearts who will be happy to help make your office cleaner, less cluttered, and more earth friendly. This Green Office challenge will bring your team together—and show them that the company cares about more than just profits.

Environment

HealthyStart

Energize together

The Healthy Start Challenge invites you to start each work day by gathering your team together for a quick group activity. Set a time like 8:50 AM before any meetings are scheduled. If mornings don't work, consider another time like mid-afternoon when people are dragging. Gather in a common area and do something invigorating, such as stretches, jumping jacks, singing, or meditation. Find an energetic person who can lead the activity and get everyone excited about it. The activity can change over time—see what your team likes and let it evolve.

On the surface, this challenge may seem corny, but it's actually quite normal in other parts of the world, like Japan, where employees routinely exercise together first thing in the morning. It's a subtle way to make sure everyone shows up to work on time and a great way to feel a sense of unity with your team. As a bonus, if your activity includes some form of stretching, it will be a boost for workplace wellness and safety. Image having your team energized and at maximum productivity right from the start of each day!

Environment

Relationships

Meetings 101

Learn how to run a meeting

Mastery

Environment

The Meetings 101 Challenge invites you to hold a training session for everyone in your area about how to run a meeting. You can plan and conduct the training or delegate it to others. Come up with a set of guidelines for running a meeting to present at the session. Search the Internet for insight if you need it—it shouldn't be hard to find materials that suit your organization. Perhaps even create a simple document with meeting tips you can send around and/or post on conference room walls. The training should only take 30–60 minutes. The principles should be simple, but powerful.

We may spend hours in meetings every week, but the time doesn't necessarily equal effectiveness. The efficiency of those meetings can skyrocket and the time spent in them can be dramatically reduced if your team knows how to run a good meeting. Simple steps like having an agenda, documenting action items, and taking time to follow up at the beginning of the next meeting can be game changers. Doing the training together will make it easier to implement the new meeting guidelines. Think of all the time you'll save!

Nice**Digs**
Improve your work environment

The Nice Digs Challenge invites you to make your work environment a more enjoyable place to be, a place where everyone can feel more at home. The changes you make can take any form: set up a break room, add artwork, improve workstation ergonomics with new keyboards or chairs, place some plants around the office, offer desk lights to provide soft light, or set up a meditation or workout area. Of course there are limits to what's possible or appropriate for your office, but you can definitely find some way to improve the space.

We spend so much of our lives at work. We might as well make it as pleasant as possible. While we can't control all aspects of the work experience, the physical environment is one of the easier elements to mold. If you think about it, the physical environment sets the tone from the moment you walk into the office—is this a fun place to be or a sterile work environment? Small things can make a huge difference. In fact, instead of making one major change, it may be more effective to implement several smaller changes over time so people constantly sense that things are improving.

Environment

PowerOn

Energize others

Communication

The Power On Challenge invites you to energize at least one person a day for the next 30 days. If you miss a day, energize two people the following day. You may be wondering what in the world it means to "energize" someone. To understand this concept, think of the interactions you've had with other people in the last 24 hours. Who increased your level of energy and who may have diminished it? What did the person do who increased or drained your energy? Your goal is to be the person who energizes other people, especially your employees. Remember, not everyone is energized in the same way.

Boosting someone else's energy may be as simple as giving them a big smile or taking the time to meaningfully understand how they are doing. It may be giving them a compliment or high-fiving them for a recent accomplishment. Hopefully this will get you in the habit of considering whether you positively or negatively impacted the energy level of each person you encounter each day. There is great power in energizing others; just like a power switch, it turns things on.

Environment

Relationships

QuietHour

Set aside an hour with no meetings

The Quiet Hour Challenge invites you to set a time one or more days a week where no meetings will be scheduled for your area and everyone is able to work quietly. Send out an invite for the Quiet Hour to block out that time on everyone's calendar as a reminder. Make the Quiet Hour a time when it's fine to close office doors, and ask those working in open areas to speak softly or not at all. The idea is to provide a time when people can focus on their work without interruption, increasing productivity and job satisfaction.

In many companies, it's the norm for everyone's calendar to be booked solid for weeks at a time. This leads to an environment where people go from meeting to meeting, squeezing in emails between or during meetings with no time to actually do any quality work. Not only does this hurt productivity, it hurts morale. The human brain needs time each day to slow down, focus, and accomplish something of depth, something of value. You'll be amazed at the positive shifts that will take place in your office when you consciously take a break from meetings.

Environment

Quiet**Zone**

Designate a quiet workplace

QUIET ZONE

The Quiet Zone Challenge invites you to designate an area where people can work without being interrupted. Pick a conference room or a lounge with enough space for several people to work. Set some simple rules for the Quiet Zone, like (1) no talking, and (2) no disturbing others when they're in the Quiet Zone. You could even create a "Quiet Zone" sign with the rules listed as a reminder. If employees are enjoying this quiet space, you may want to set up regular workstations with monitors, or even standing desks. If you can't afford to give up a conference room completely, consider scheduling it for a set number of hours each day to use as a Quiet Zone.

Most workspaces today have open seating, which is great for collaboration, but can get noisy and distracting at times. Offering a Quiet Zone can provide the best of both worlds—the ability for a team to work in close proximity while also encouraging individuals to concentrate on their own independent efforts. It also shows employees that you value them and their occasional need to work in a silent and focused manner. Silence is golden!

Thank**First**

Begin 20 meetings with gratitude

The Thank First Challenge invites you to begin 20 meetings by expressing your appreciation for those in attendance. The meetings can have hundreds of attendees or be a simple one-on-one. On the surface, it may sound like it would be awkward, but it doesn't have to be. Find a way to include an expression of gratitude in the meeting kickoff. Get beyond the basic, "I'm grateful that you have taken your time to be here today." Use words that specifically connect with those people you address so they know how truly thankful you are.

So often we rush into a meeting anxious to accomplish our objectives, treating people like objects—things that are in our way instead of partners who can help us accomplish our goal. This simple practice of expressing gratitude at the start of a meeting will help shift your mindset and hopefully the mindset of the others in the room from self-centeredness to collaboration. This can lay the groundwork for you to harness the power of cooperation and accomplish things normally not possible. How will your expression of gratitude affect your attendees' attitude?

Environment

Vital**Statistics**

Conduct a survey

The Vital Statistics Challenge invites you to conduct a survey, which can be on any topic, for any audience. Conduct a survey to help improve the work you do. Create a survey to help design the holiday party. Survey people internally or survey your customers or suppliers. As you write your questions for the survey, consider what you want from the results. Make sure to include open-ended questions to collect information that numbers don't. Many people are surveyed too frequently, so choose your target audience carefully and keep it brief. Consider a test run before distributing the real survey. Feel free to delegate all or part of this work to your team—including the creation of the survey itself.

A survey can be a great tool to gather information that will help you improve your business. Simply asking for feedback and ideas can be quite revealing. In addition to general feedback, surveys offer the power of hard data that you may be able to use later on. There's nothing like a chart with precise numbers to support an idea you are trying to promote. What can be even more interesting is year-over-year changes in the data. To get that, however, you'll need to gather data for your first year. So get started today!

WarmUp

Start 3 meetings with a fun activity

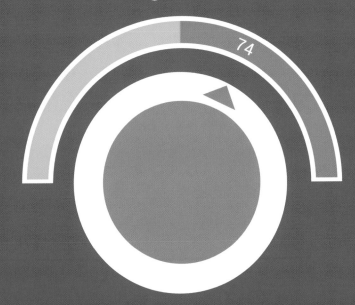

The Warm Up Challenge invites you to start three meetings with something different, fun, or thought-provoking. Anything goes! Ask everyone in the room to say something they're grateful for. Watch a funny or inspirational video. Have someone play their favorite song and explain why it's their favorite. Hold a one-minute treasure hunt. Pass around a snack or treat. Whatever it is, try to keep it to five minutes or less—you don't want to derail the entire meeting! If you're having trouble thinking of ideas, ask around, or search the Internet.

A fun activity at the beginning of a meeting may seem like a waste of time, but it can actually be an accelerator to greater things. It can energize everyone and get them thinking. It can break down barriers and make everyone more willing to share ideas. It can spur creativity and get people thinking out of the box. It simply makes work fun—and who doesn't like to have a little fun? How will you start your next meeting?

Environment

Full**House**

Hold a family event

The Full House Challenge invites you to hold a work event that includes the families or housemates of your employees. Plan a summer picnic. Have a dinner night with games at the office. Go to a fun center. Have a Halloween party. The event can be any activity that gives everyone a chance to meet each other's friends and families. Brainstorm ideas with your team and ask for a volunteer to plan the event with the help of a committee.

Having a chance to meet your coworkers' loved ones helps you connect with them on a more personal level. You realize that Shannon is a mom who loves and nurtures her two little children. You find out that Bob volunteers as a coach for his son's soccer team, Jenni is about to get engaged to her boyfriend, and Jake's mom just moved in with his family. You understand that work is only a small part of each coworker's life. As people learn more about each other, they will treat each other with more compassion and understanding—and we all could use some more of that when the going gets tough!

HeadChef

Cook for your team

The Head Chef Challenge invites you to cook something for your team. You could simply bake cookies, but see if you can go beyond that. Prepare a healthy snack like a fruit cup in the morning or fresh guacamole and chips in the afternoon. Have some fun and set aside some time for people to critique your food, like on a cooking show. Go big and prepare lunch or invite the team over to your house for dinner. If cooking's not your thing, ask someone to help you figure out something that would work. You can also ask for help preparing the food, but the more you do yourself, the more impactful it will be.

Cooking is a way to serve others and show them they're important to you, you appreciate them, and you don't think that you are better than them. This simple activity opens the door for providing your employees with other, more meaningful types of service. Of course, as a manager, you're not supposed to spend your day doing everyone's work for them. However, you can still serve them as you work to help them become successful—serving them as a coach instead of a drill sergeant. You will become a better manager as you become a better servant.

Environment

Relationships

Head**Coach**

Mentor someone

Communication

Collaboration

Relationships

The Head Coach Challenge invites you to conduct three mentoring sessions with one person from your organization. Switching things up from the norm, you get to choose whom you mentor. Pick someone you'd like to groom for the future or whom you think would enjoy the mentoring process. When approaching this person about a possible mentor relationship, it wouldn't hurt to point out the potential you see in them, and your desire to help them grow in a way you know is possible. If they're not interested, choose another candidate.

Mentoring can be as formal or informal as you like. In the first meeting, either one of you could bring a list of topics to discuss or you could let the conversation take its own course. Even though you've initiated the mentoring, resist the temptation to give out unsolicited advice since most people don't like to be told what to do. Instead, listen and ask thought-provoking questions and wait for the person to ask for advice. Your support will definitely make an impact, and both of you will benefit equally! Relationships are important and mentoring is a great way to build them.

KidDay

Sponsor a children-at-work day

The Kid Day Challenge invites you to sponsor a day for employees to bring a child to work. Your organization may already support the nationally recognized Take Our Daughters and Sons to Work Day. If so, actively promote it to your group so everyone feels comfortable participating. If not, create your own unofficial program and invite employees to bring a child (not necessarily theirs) to work—either on a specific day or any day throughout the year. Create an expectation that the child can participate in the workday by attending meetings and performing small tasks.

The most obvious goal of this initiative is to allow children to start exploring careers at a young age, but there are so many other benefits for the workplace. Think how healthy it is for workers to share the people they love the most with their coworkers—a gentle reminder why everyone goes to work in the first place. Seeing coworkers with children also humanizes them—reminding everyone that they are real people who care deeply for others, not an object that is in someone else's way at work. It may slow things down on that particular workday, but in the long term, productivity will be much higher and your employees will be happier.

Environment

Relationships

LunchLotto
Organize random lunch dates

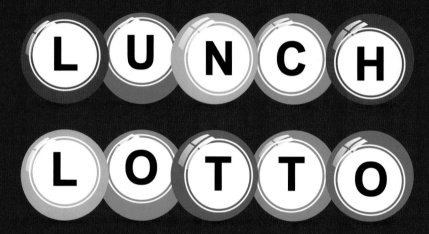

The Lunch Lotto Challenge invites you to set up lunch dates between random people in your organization. Randomly select groups of three people to go to lunch together to promote new relationships. If you have the funds, pay for the lunches—everyone loves a free lunch! If you don't have the budget to cover the lunches and need to ask the employees to pay, make sure they know that in advance and that participation is optional. Once the groups are determined, let them choose where and when they would like to do lunch—or assign lunch destinations in a lotto fashion too!

The goal of this challenge is to build relationships, the oil that greases the work environment. If your organization has weak relationships, there will be friction and possible overheating at times. If it has strong relationships, things will go smoothly even when the pressure is on. When people have strong connections with their coworkers, they enjoy being at work more and will have greater longevity with the company. Help build those relationships by organizing your Lunch Lotto today!

Lunch Time

Have 6 lunches

The Lunch Time Challenge invites you to have six lunches with people in your organization. Grab a quick bite or enjoy a relaxing, hour-long lunch together. If you don't have a budget for things like this, go for coffee instead or ask people if they are okay paying for their own lunch—something they may be happy to do to have some quality time with you. Work topics will probably come up, but do your best to spend time talking about non-work topics so you can get to know everyone on a more personal level. If you're a talker, hold back a bit to let the others talk so you can get to know them better.

Having lunch with others is a great way to recharge in the middle of the day. On the surface, it may not seem like a constructive use of time, but getting to know and trust your team not only helps with employee retention, it helps regular work go more smoothly and quickly. Don't underestimate how much work you'll get done over lunch (even though it's technically not a business lunch). As you all sit back and relax, ideas will come and conversations will take place that never would have happened back at the office. Make work a little more fun for everyone and plan your lunches today!

NameGame
Learn 10 names

The Name Game Challenge invites you to learn the names of 10 family members of your employees. You hear the names of their family members mentioned all the time, but you probably only have a few committed to memory. To help you remember, write the names down as well as any particular details, like age or hobbies to help you keep them straight. Try to learn the name of a family member for each person in your area, especially their spouse or significant other.

Remembering someone's name shows that they are important to you. Remembering the names of their family members is also meaningful, but much more powerful. It shows you realize they have a life outside of work, there are other things that are much more important to them than work, and most likely more dear to them than anything else. Knowing these names is a launching point for conversations that go deeper than the weather or last night's game. Take the time to learn family names and show your employees how much you care!

PhotoWall

Post employee pictures

The Photo Wall Challenge invites you to designate a wall in your office where people can post informal pictures of themselves. Make it easy by allowing people to tape or pin up pictures on the wall—even pictures straight off the printer. Until there are several pictures posted, people may be hesitant to participate, so you may have to solicit people individually or designate a launch date for everyone to post their photos together. Once it's going, people will be much more willing to add to it. If your team is geographically distributed, use an online tool to create a virtual wall.

A photo wall is a fun way for people to share what's going on in their lives—and for others to find out what they're up to. It will spark many conversations and will unite everyone as they view and enjoy each other's photos. It will also help everyone remember there is more to life than work. Find a place for your photo wall and watch how it brings people together.

Environment

Relationships

Pot**Luck**

Hold a potluck

The Pot Luck Challenge invites you to organize a potluck for your group—breakfast, lunch, dinner, or even snacks! You could ask for a volunteer to organize it—then all you have to do is bring something to share. However, this is a good challenge for you to organize yourself. It's pretty simple. Just choose a date, time, and location. If you want to ensure variety, create a sign-up sheet with categories (e.g., main dish, salad, side, dessert). Consider a theme for the event around healthy foods, ethnic foods, or family favorites.

A potluck provides a unique opportunity for people to get to know each other better. Many people love to share their favorite foods. Of course some will just check the box and bring normal fare, but others will go to great lengths to prepare the food they bring—and they'll be delighted to tell you all about it! Another option is to have everyone bring printed copies of the recipes they've made. Enjoy a meal together and get to know your group better. If you haven't had a potluck within the last year, you're missing out!

Rough Times

Help someone having a hard time

The Rough Times Challenge invites you to band together as a team and help someone who is going through a challenging time or life-altering situation. It could be any struggle—like an illness, death, flood, fire, divorce, birth, marriage, or move. If there's no one on your team facing a challenge, look outside your team or wait until you see a need. Make sure the person is okay with others knowing their situation. What you choose to do to help will depend on the situation. It may be as simple as sending flowers, signing a card, or collecting money. Take turns bringing in meals, offer to babysit, or simply spend time talking with the person. In this potentially sensitive situation, an employee-led effort will feel better.

Focusing on helping a person in your organization will bring a sense of humanity to the office. It is a good reminder that everyone goes through tough times, even though it may not show on the outside. Offering someone a little bit of kindness can lighten their load. Joining together to help another person can unify your work team and soften their hearts so they treat each other with more kindness and patience. Also, focusing on others' rough times helps everyone put the daily problems of the workplace into perspective, making your workplace more effective!

Relationships

SantaClaus

Give gifts to your team

The Santa Claus Challenge invites you to give gifts to your team members. You can give everyone the same gift or give different ones. The value of the gift is not as important as the thought that goes into it. A favorite treat, flowers, or a premium cup of coffee can make someone's day and let them know that you care about them. Make it even more special by wrapping the gift and/or including a card with some kind words. The more thought you put into it, the more powerful the experience will be for you and the recipient—so try to stay away from gift cards!

The act of giving is a powerful tool. Done properly it turns your focus outward, forcing you to think about what others would really like. As you better understand the needs of others, it will change your outlook, calm your soul, and multiply your effectiveness. On the flip side, those who receive your gifts will be very appreciative. They'll be more willing to roll with the punches and see you as a regular person instead of just an authority figure. Experience the joy that Santa Claus does and start giving today!

Environment

Relationships

Servant**Leader**

Serve 5 people

The Servant Leader Challenge invites you to serve those who work for you—five people to be exact. This may take some creativity on your part and may even be a little awkward, but it will be worth it. Complete some unpleasant paperwork for them, help them with a presentation, or offer to pick up lunch for them when they're in crunch mode. If you can't think of anything, just ask what you can do (filling them in about the challenge if you'd like). As awkward as it may be at the moment, it will leave an impression.

True leaders serve those they lead. Performing little acts of service for your team helps you remember that you are no better than they are and only happen to be serving the role of leader— one of many important roles. Make a conscious effort to put the interests of others above your own. Do yourself and your group a favor and show them you're there to serve them!

Serve**Together**

Serve the community

The Serve Together Challenge invites you to organize a service event for your community. Organize it yourself or have someone on your team take charge. There are plenty of service organizations looking for help; ask around if you need ideas. Choose a project that you can work on together as a team so there will be opportunities for bonding and unity. If you're worried about attendance, hold the event during work hours and end with a happy hour. Don't rush getting this going. Keep working the idea until you find one that you feel good about.

A service event can be a huge help to the community, and also provide invaluable benefits for your team. It provides an opportunity for employees to build relationships outside the work environment and shows that your company cares and wants to give back. Make sure you personally work at the event or it will show just the opposite about you! Another great benefit is on a personal level: Each person who serves others will gain a new perspective and feel gratitude for what they have, including their job and those they work with. Serving together is so powerful that you may want to consider making it a tradition for your team!

SocialButterflies

Have a team outing

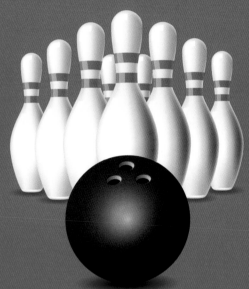

The Social Butterflies Challenge invites you to sponsor a company event outside the office with your team. Go bowling, try an escape room, or maybe a round of minigolf. Pick something that will appeal to everyone on your team. If your team is not into late evening activities, plan a lunch out or end work early and go out for appetizers. Whatever you plan, make sure it gives them the chance to socialize. If budget is an issue, choose something without cost, like kickball or Frisbee in the park. If you don't enjoy planning activities, ask someone on your team who does to coordinate the activity.

Interacting outside the work environment can pay dividends. Not only is it fun and a release from work, it brings you together as a team by creating positive memories. It also creates an opportunity for people to see another side of their work associates and understand each other better. Once everyone is back at work, the fun memories and strengthened relationships will help people be more forgiving and understanding of each other. Productivity will increase while tension will go down. What type of outing would your team enjoy?

Relationships

Story Time

Tell 3 stories

The Story Time Challenge invites you to tell three stories to inspire your team or to make a particular point. The stories can be your own personal stories, ones you've read, or ones you've heard others tell. Tell the stories in meetings or in one-on-one conversations. Ideally, tell them at work, but you can also share them in your personal life. If you're having a hard time coming up with stories to share, pick a setting for storytelling first—an upcoming meeting or event—then try to think of a story that would be appropriate. If you're still struggling, explain the purpose of the meeting to a friend and see if they can come up with a story you could use.

Intuitively, you may think facts, figures, and logic are needed to make a point—and they often are—but they do a poor job winning the hearts of others. Stories grab people's attention, convey emotion, and are much easier to remember. Whether you're trying to sell a product, convince your team to make a change, or connect on a deeper level...stories are the way to go!

TrueFeeling

Ask 10 people how they feel

The True Feeling Challenge invites you to ask 10 people how they feel in a general sense or how they feel about something specific, like their job or a particular situation. It's important you ask them specifically how they "feel," not just how they are doing. Start your conversation as you normally would, then progress to asking how they feel. If your first try doesn't spur a heartfelt response, reword your question to let them know you're truly interested. Perhaps most important, be sure to listen attentively and ask follow-up questions. Resist the temptation to negate their thoughts—feelings are always true for the person having them.

So often we go through life exchanging shallow pleasantries, engaging in small talk, but never sharing the true feelings of our heart. When we share our feelings, we connect with associates at a much deeper level. We'll build stronger relationships, which will make work more enjoyable, reduce conflict, and help us get through rough times. You might think you don't have enough time to do this, but you already take time to talk with others. Simply shift the focus of your conversations and make them deeper and more meaningful.

WalkAround

Manage by walking around

Communication

Collaboration

Relationships

The Walk Around Challenge invites you to spend 15 minutes each day at work mingling with others—especially those in your group—over the next 30 days. Walk around the office first thing in the morning, in between meetings, or whenever you need a break. Look for someone you haven't talked with for a while. Spend five minutes with three people or 15 minutes with one person. Whether you talk about work or your personal lives—it really doesn't matter. The important thing is that you are taking time to connect with others to better understand them as real people, not just employees.

President Theodore Roosevelt once said, "Nobody cares how much you know, until they know how much you care." Walking around the office and taking time to be with people will help show them how much you care. It's also a great way to learn how to care *more*. As we take the time to understand others, our hearts will soften toward them and our empathy will grow. You'll be amazed at how many of your conversations will result in action, bringing forth new plans or ideas that wouldn't have sprung forth otherwise, all because you took the time to talk with another person.